# DESTINATION X

**JOHN MARTZ**

NOBROW PRESS

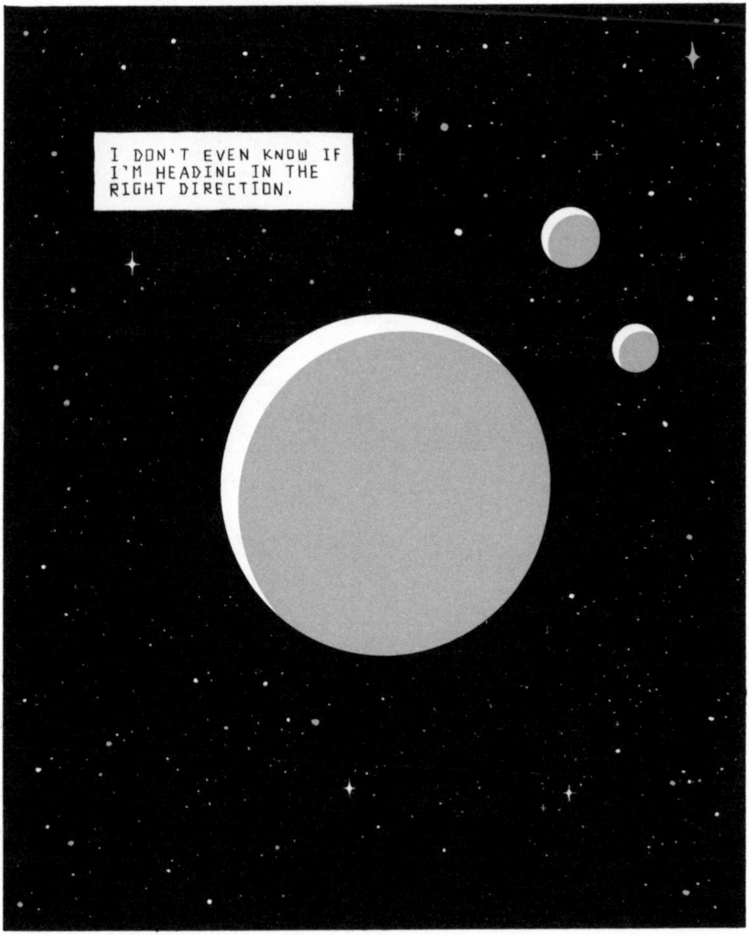
I DON'T EVEN KNOW IF I'M HEADING IN THE RIGHT DIRECTION.

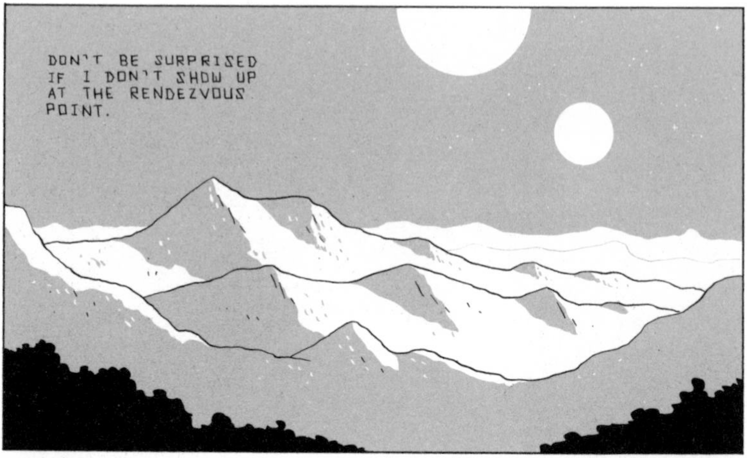
DON'T BE SURPRISED IF I DON'T SHOW UP AT THE RENDEZVOUS POINT.

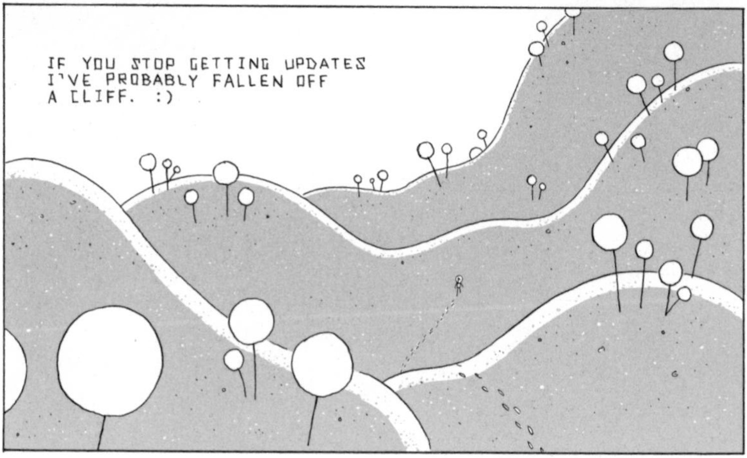
IF YOU STOP GETTING UPDATES I'VE PROBABLY FALLEN OFF A CLIFF. :)

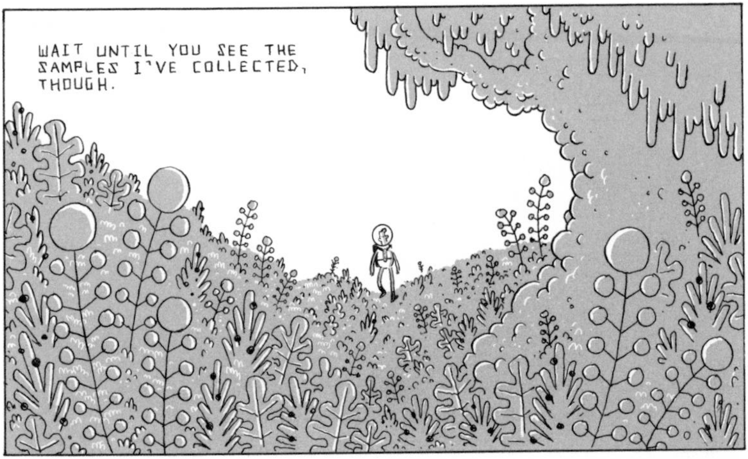
WAIT UNTIL YOU SEE THE SAMPLES I'VE COLLECTED, THOUGH.

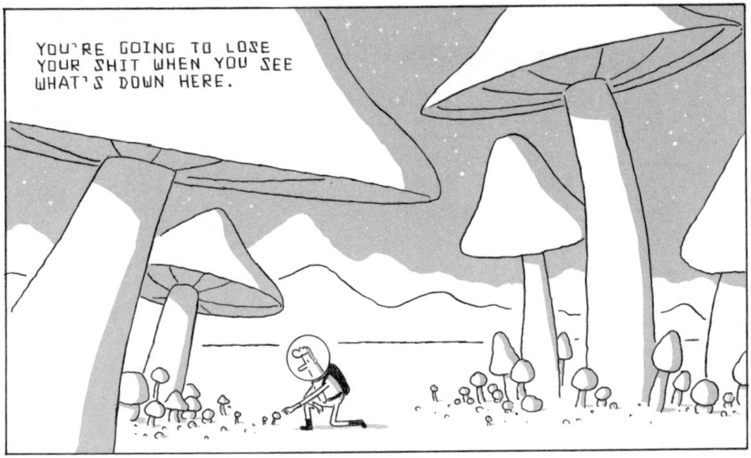
YOU'RE GOING TO LOSE YOUR SHIT WHEN YOU SEE WHAT'S DOWN HERE.

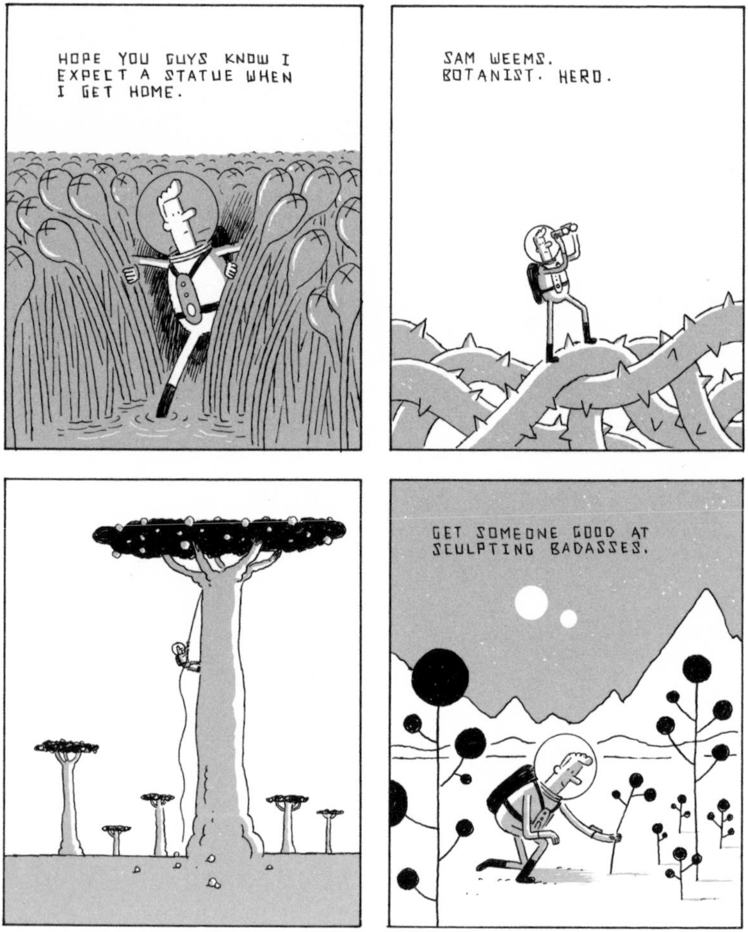
HOPE YOU GUYS KNOW I EXPECT A STATUE WHEN I GET HOME.
SAM WEEMS. BOTANIST. HERO.
GET SOMEONE GOOD AT SCULPTING BADASSES.

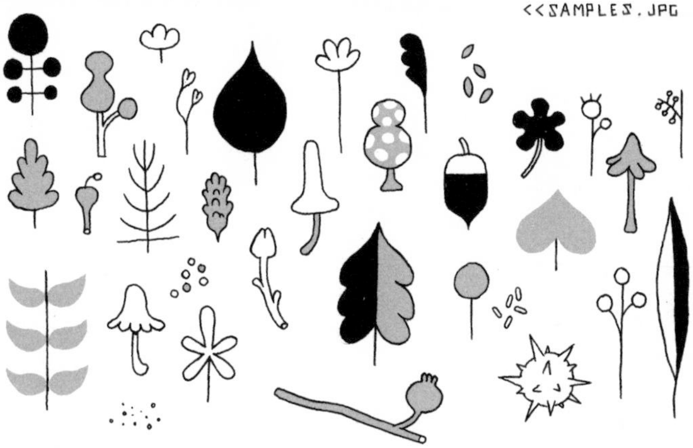
<<SAMPLES.JPG

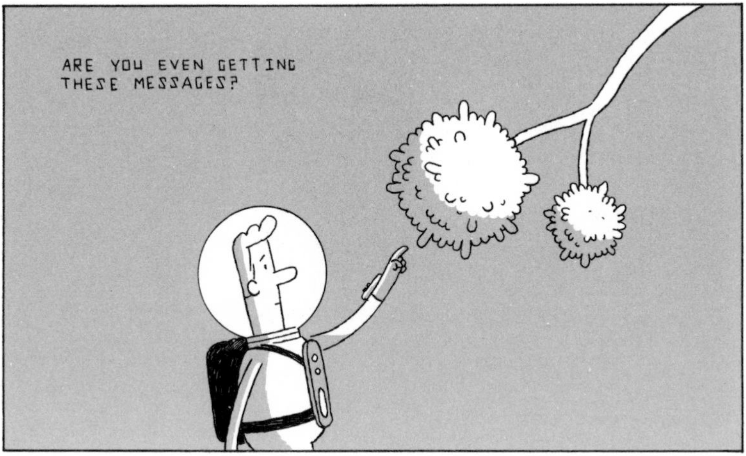
ARE YOU EVEN GETTING
THESE MESSAGES?

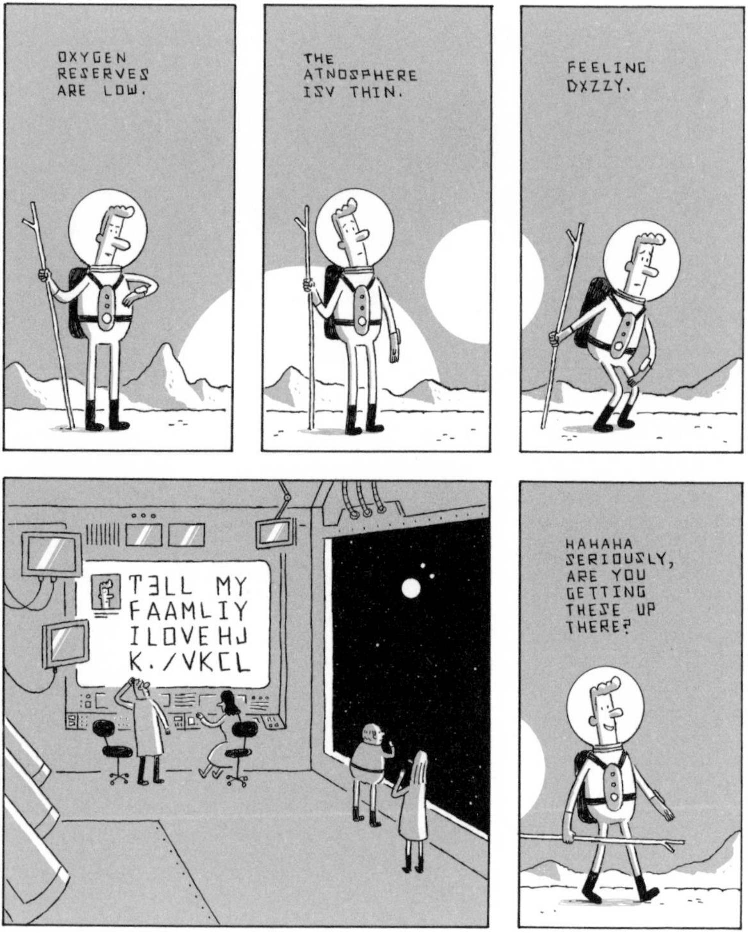
OXYGEN RESERVES ARE LOW.
THE ATNOSPHERE ISV THIN.
FEELING DXZZY.
T3LL MY FAAMLIY ILOVE HJ K./VKCL
HAHAHA SERIOUSLY, ARE YOU GETTING THESE UP THERE?

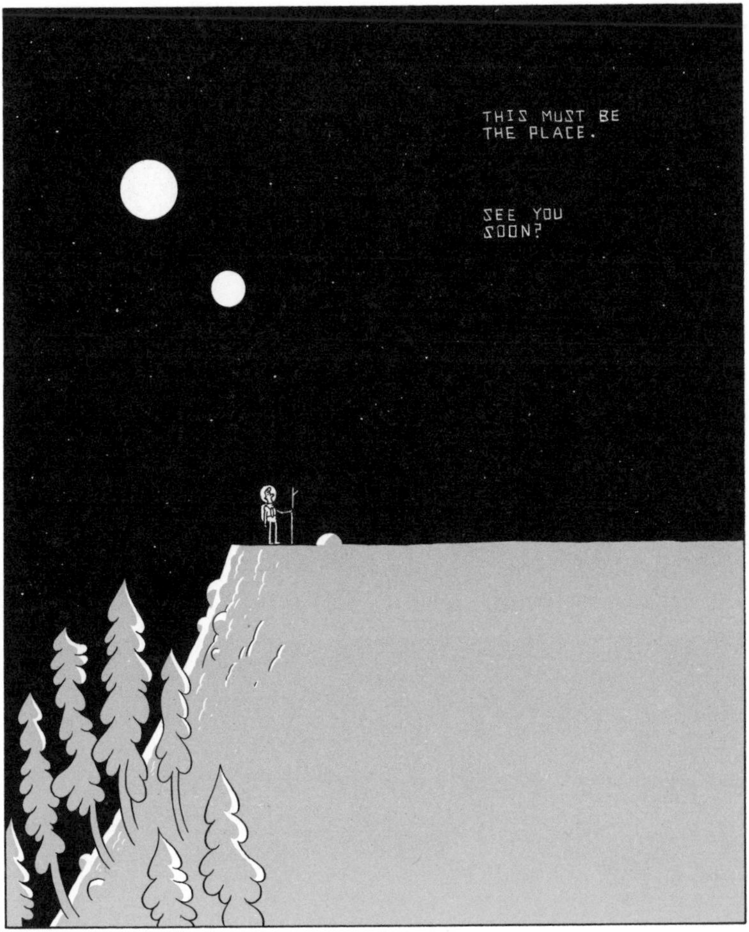
THIS MUST BE THE PLACE.
SEE YOU SOON?

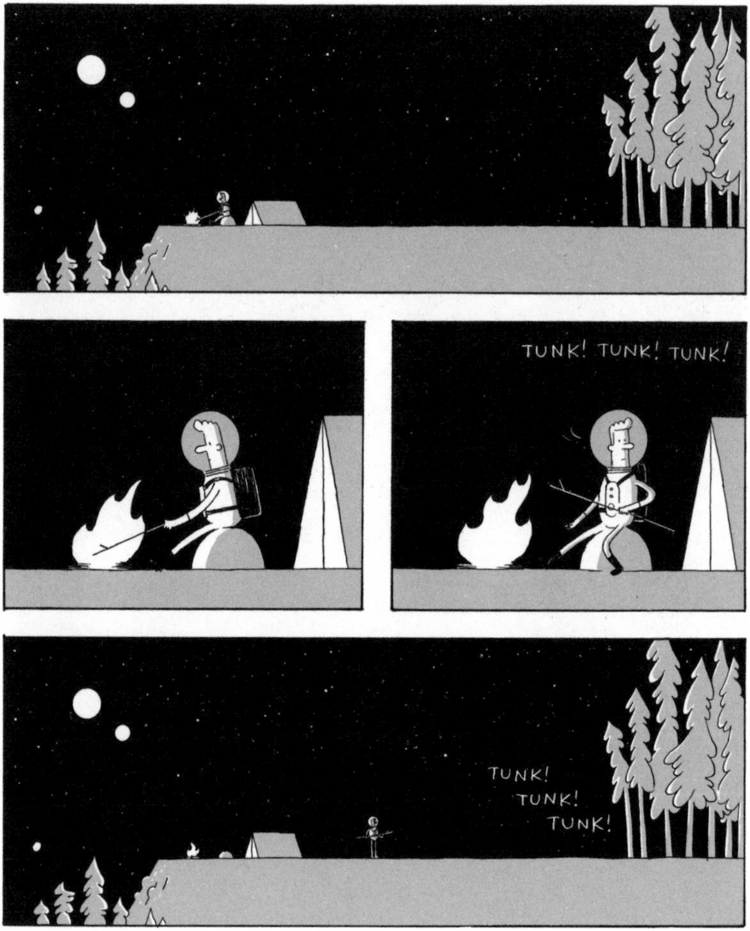
TUNK! TUNK! TUNK!
TUNK!
TUNK!
TUNK!

HELLO?
TUNK!

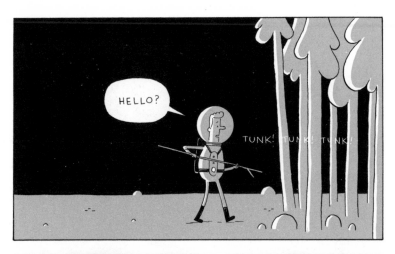

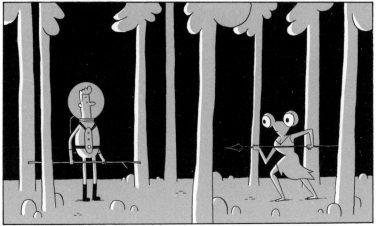

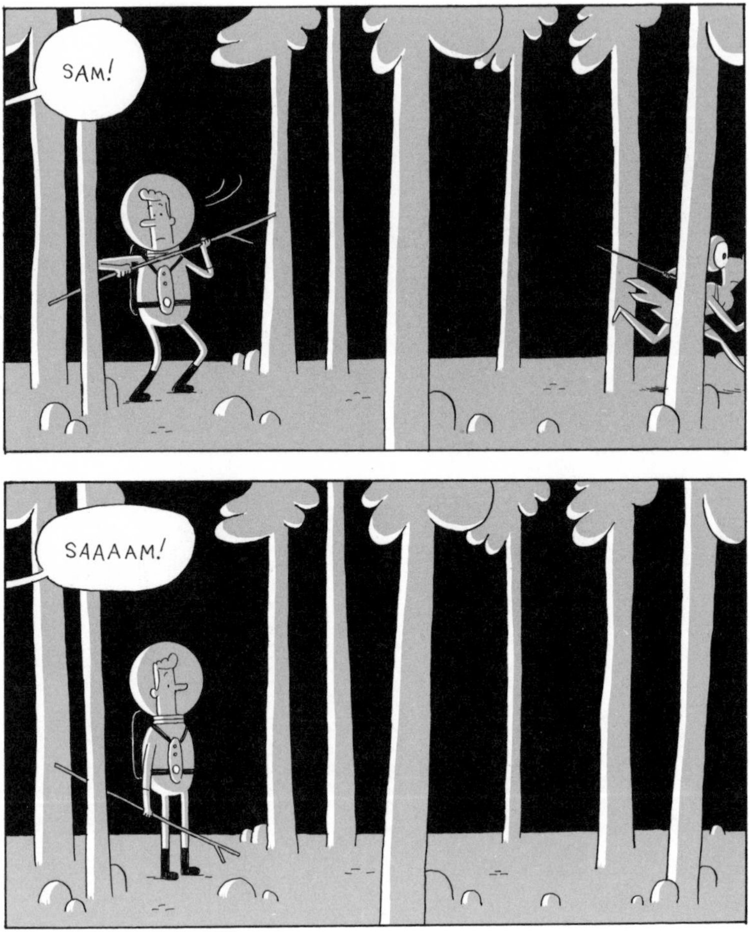
SAM!
SAAAAM!

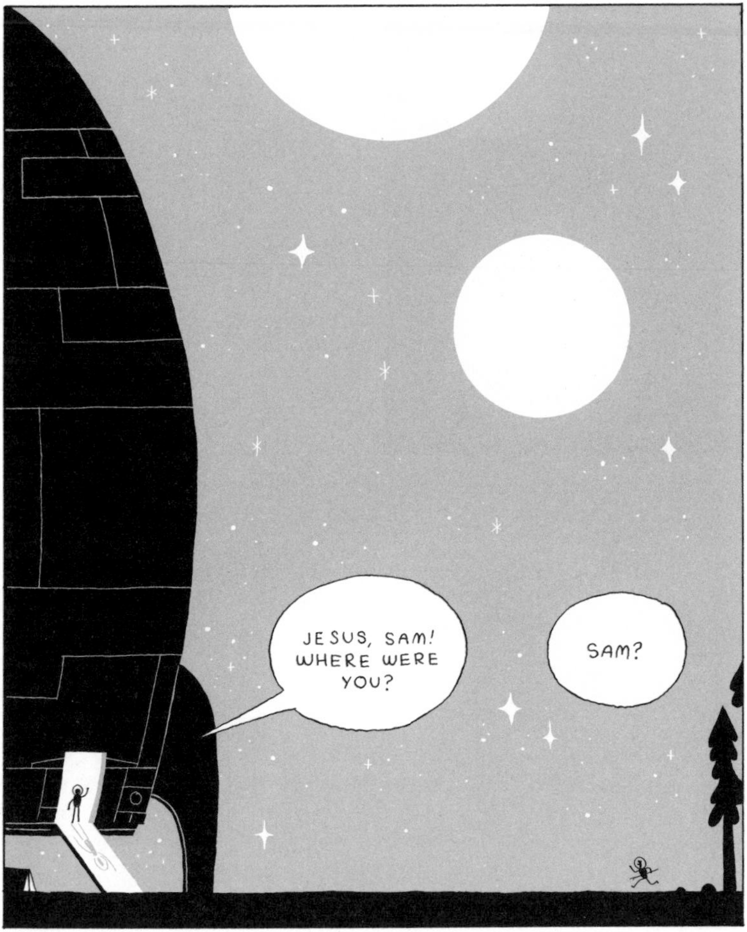
JESUS, SAM! WHERE WERE YOU?
SAM?

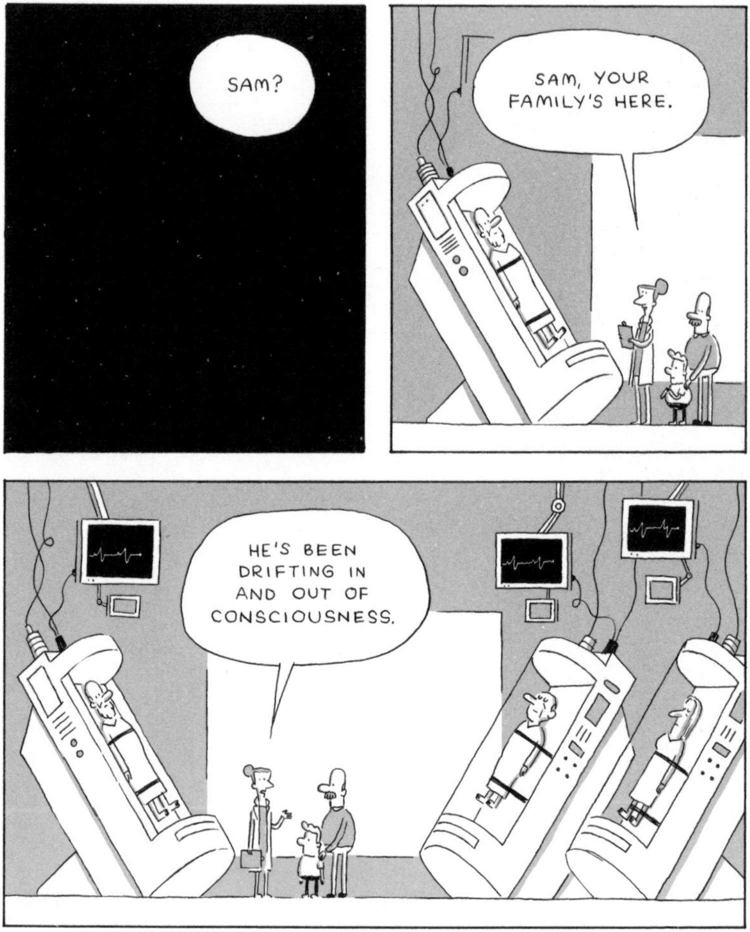
SAM?
SAM, YOUR FAMILY'S HERE.
HE'S BEEN DRIFTING IN AND OUT OF CONSCIOUSNESS.

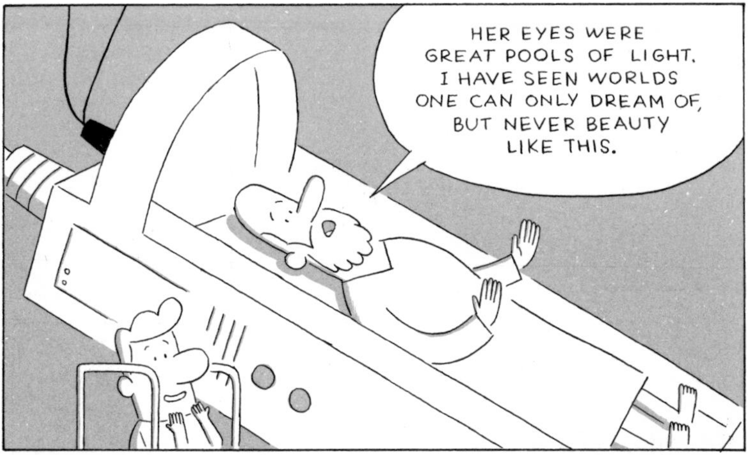
HER EYES WERE GREAT POOLS OF LIGHT. I HAVE SEEN WORLDS ONE CAN ONLY DREAM OF, BUT NEVER BEAUTY LIKE THIS.

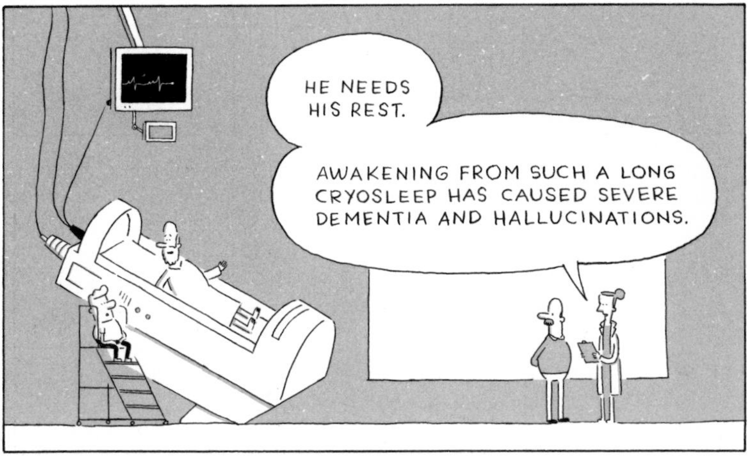
HE NEEDS HIS REST.
AWAKENING FROM SUCH A LONG CRYOSLEEP HAS CAUSED SEVERE DEMENTIA AND HALLUCINATIONS.

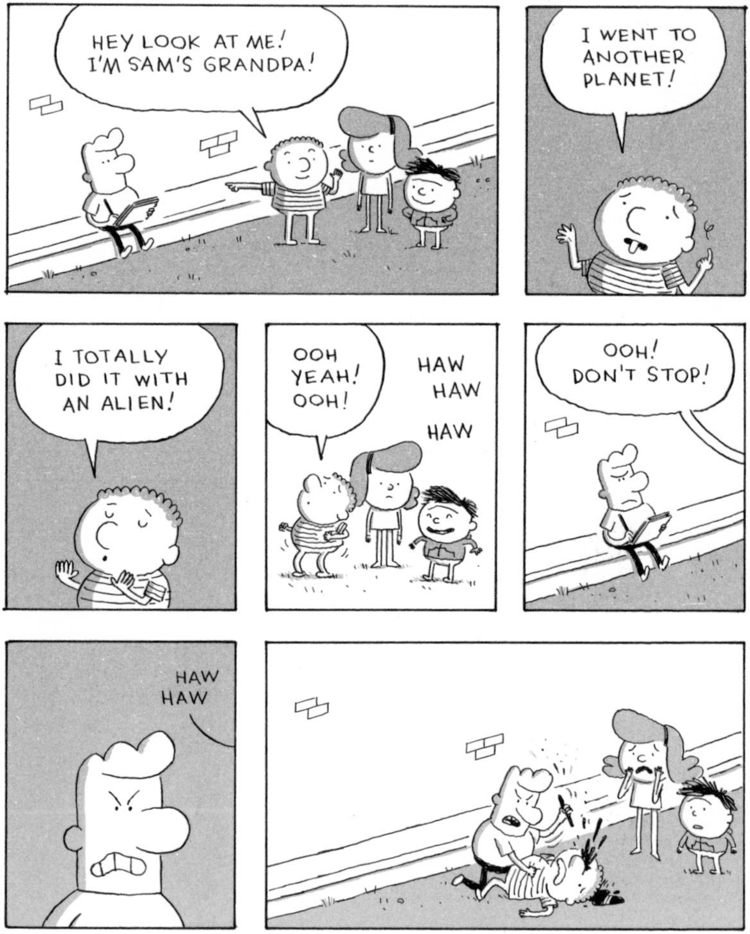
HEY LOOK AT ME! I'M SAM'S GRANDPA!
I WENT TO ANOTHER PLANET!
I TOTALLY DID IT WITH AN ALIEN!
OOH YEAH! OOH!
HAW HAW
HAW
OOH! DON'T STOP!
HAW HAW

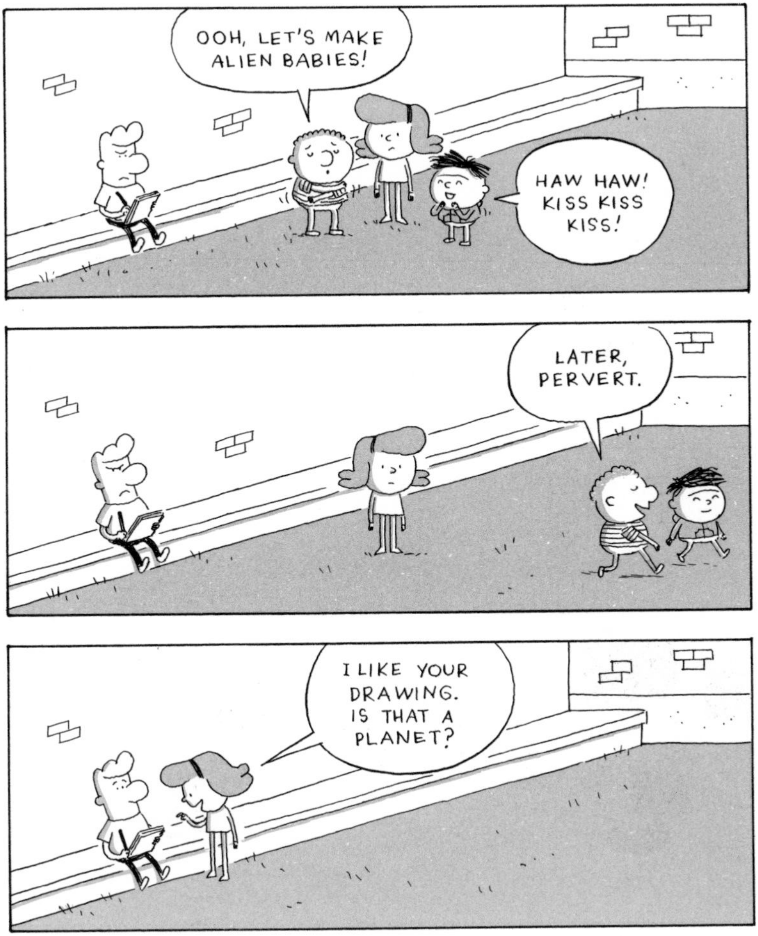
OOH, LET'S MAKE ALIEN BABIES!
HAW HAW! KISS KISS KISS!
LATER, PERVERT.
I LIKE YOUR DRAWING. IS THAT A PLANET?

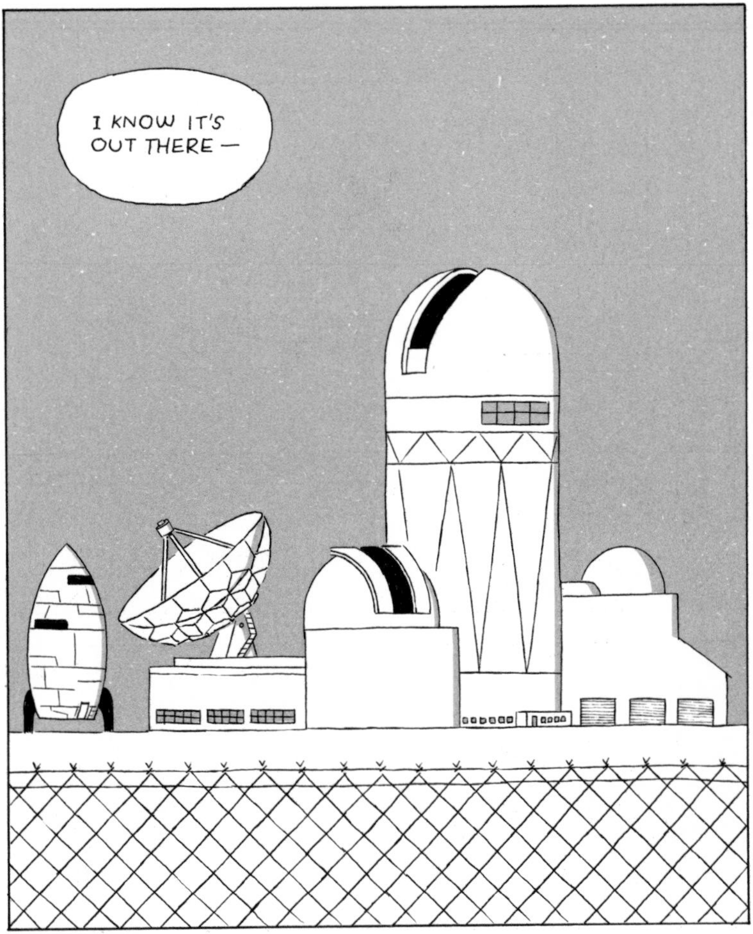
I KNOW IT'S OUT THERE —

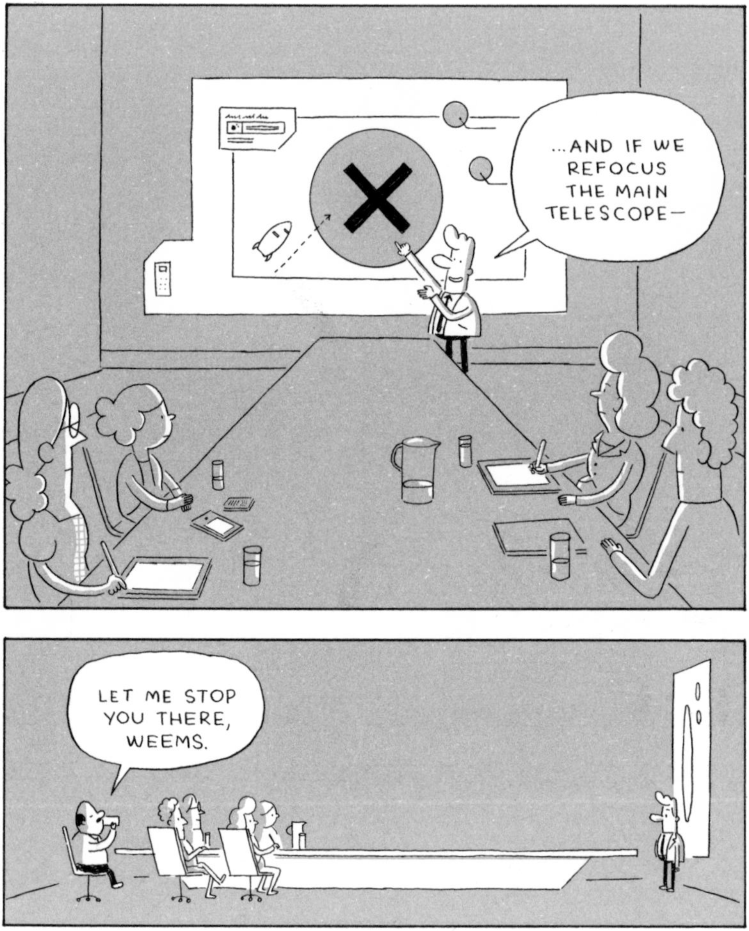
...AND IF WE REFOCUS THE MAIN TELESCOPE—
LET ME STOP YOU THERE, WEEMS.

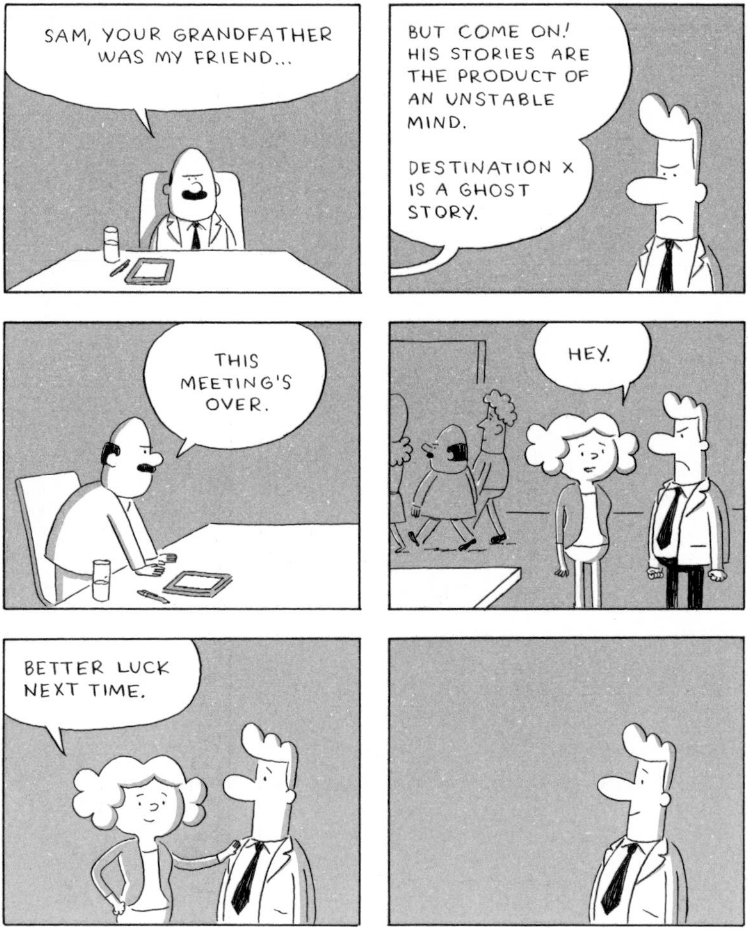
SAM, YOUR GRANDFATHER WAS MY FRIEND...
BUT COME ON! HIS STORIES ARE THE PRODUCT OF AN UNSTABLE MIND.
DESTINATION X IS A GHOST STORY.
THIS MEETING'S OVER.
HEY.
BETTER LUCK NEXT TIME.

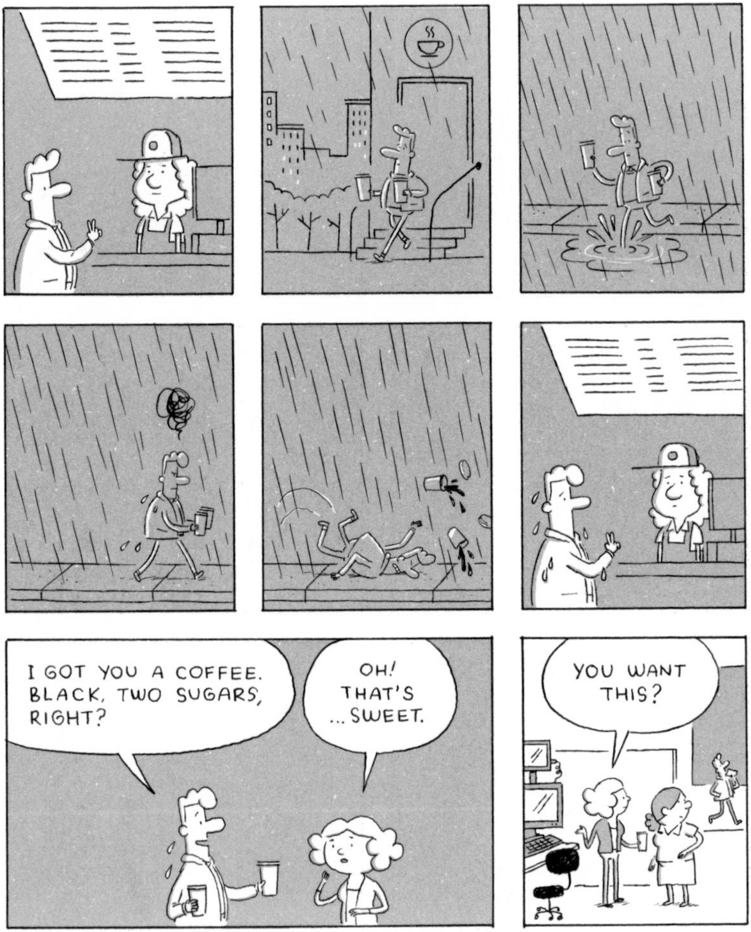
I GOT YOU A COFFEE. BLACK, TWO SUGARS, RIGHT?
OH! THAT'S ...SWEET.
YOU WANT THIS?

[Pray for me] that I will fearlessly make known
the mystery of the gospel.

# A FRIENDLY CONVERSATION

C atherine and I were good friends in high school. When we weren't talking on the phone, we were passing notes in class to plan our next sleepover. Sometimes we rode horses together and partnered on school projects.

One Sunday afternoon, I started to think about Catherine. My pastor had spoken that morning about how to have eternal life, and I knew my friend didn't believe the Bible's teachings the way I did. I felt a burden to call her and explain how she could have a relationship with Jesus. I hesitated, though, because I was afraid she would reject what I said and distance herself from me.

I think this fear keeps a lot of us quiet. Even the apostle Paul had to ask people to pray that he would "fearlessly make known the mystery of the gospel" (EPHESIANS 6:19). There's no getting around the risk involved with sharing the good news, yet Paul said he was "an ambassador"—someone speaking on behalf of God (V. 20). We are too. If people reject our message, they're also rejecting the One who sent the message. God experiences the sting along with us.

So what compels us to speak up? We care about people, like God does (2 PETER 3:9). That's what led me to finally call Catherine. Amazingly, she didn't shut me down. She listened. She asked questions. She asked Jesus to forgive her sin and decided to live for Him. The risk was worth the reward.　　　　*JENNIFER BENSON SCHULDT*

**Whom might God want you to speak to on His behalf? What's stopping you? What effect would prayer have on this situation?**

*Dear Father, give me the courage to reach out to people who don't know You. Give me wisdom to know when and how to start conversations about You.*

**BIBLE IN A YEAR** │ NUMBERS 23–25; MARK 7:14–37

FOR PERSONAL and FAMILY DEVOTIONS. *SINCE 1956*

# Our Daily Bread

## MARCH 2022

**COVER PHOTO:** *Iceland,* Terry Bidgood © Our Daily Bread Ministries

**EDITORIAL TEAM:** Paul Brinkerhoff, Tom Felten, Tim Gustafson, Regie Keller, Alyson Kieda, Becky Knapp, Monica La Rose, and Peggy Willison

**ACKNOWLEDGMENTS:** Scripture taken from Holy Bible, New International Version®, NIV® Copyright © 1973, 1978, 1984, 2011 by Biblica, Inc.® Used by permission. All rights reserved worldwide.

**VOLUME 66, NUMBER 12**

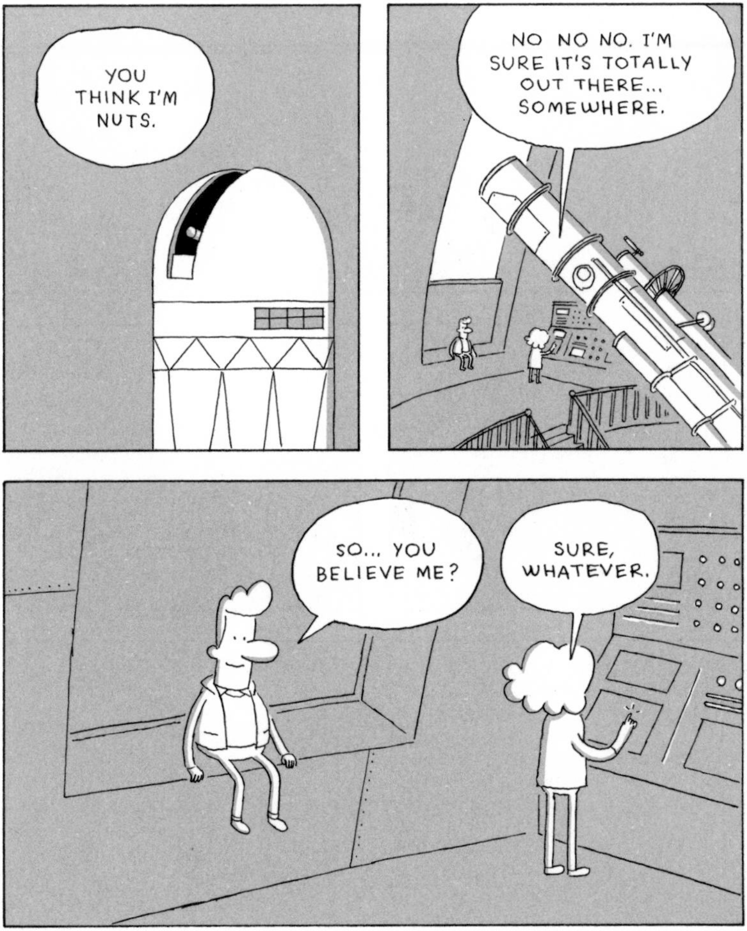
YOU THINK I'M NUTS.
NO NO NO. I'M SURE IT'S TOTALLY OUT THERE... SOMEWHERE.
SO... YOU BELIEVE ME?
SURE, WHATEVER.

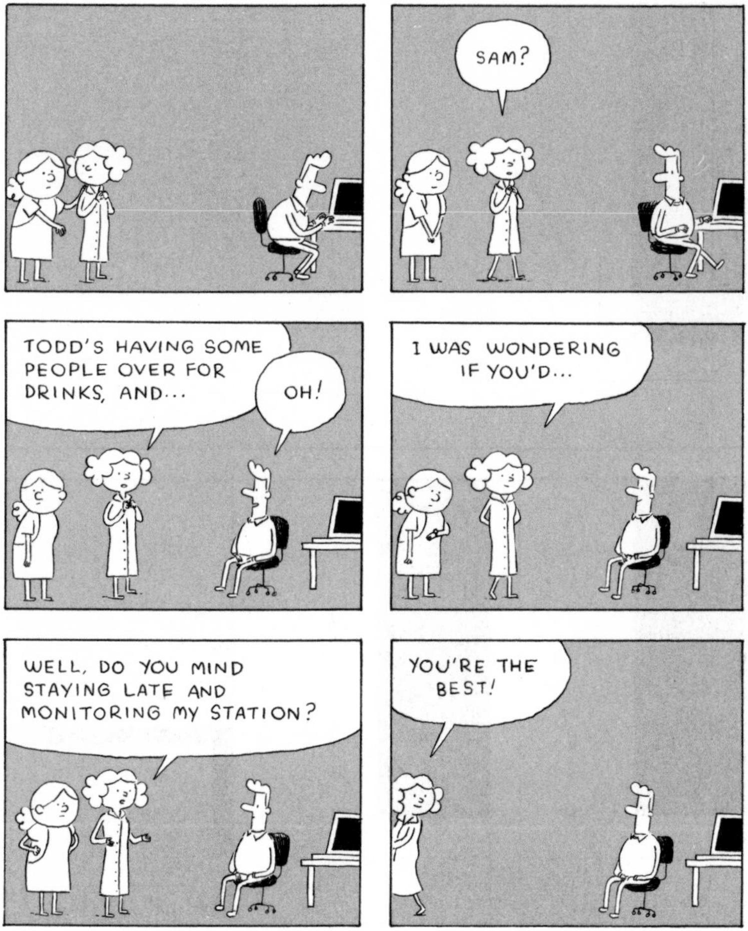
SAM?
TODD'S HAVING SOME PEOPLE OVER FOR DRINKS, AND...
OH!
I WAS WONDERING IF YOU'D...
WELL, DO YOU MIND STAYING LATE AND MONITORING MY STATION?
YOU'RE THE BEST!

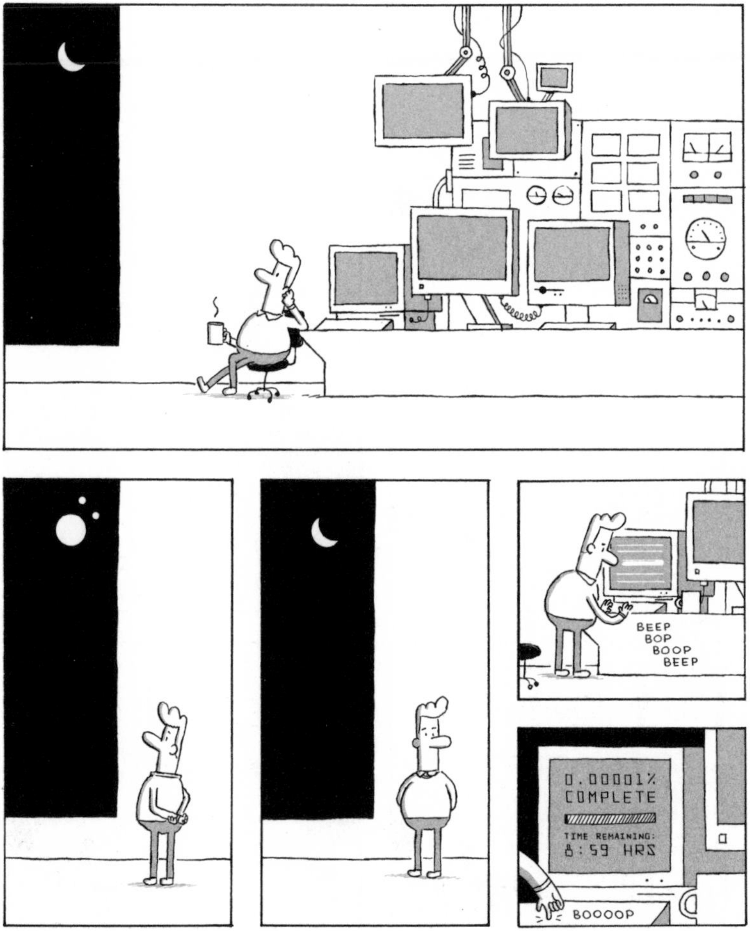
BEEP
BOP
BOOP
BEEP
0.00001%
COMPLETE
TIME REMAINING:
8:59 HRS
BOOOOP

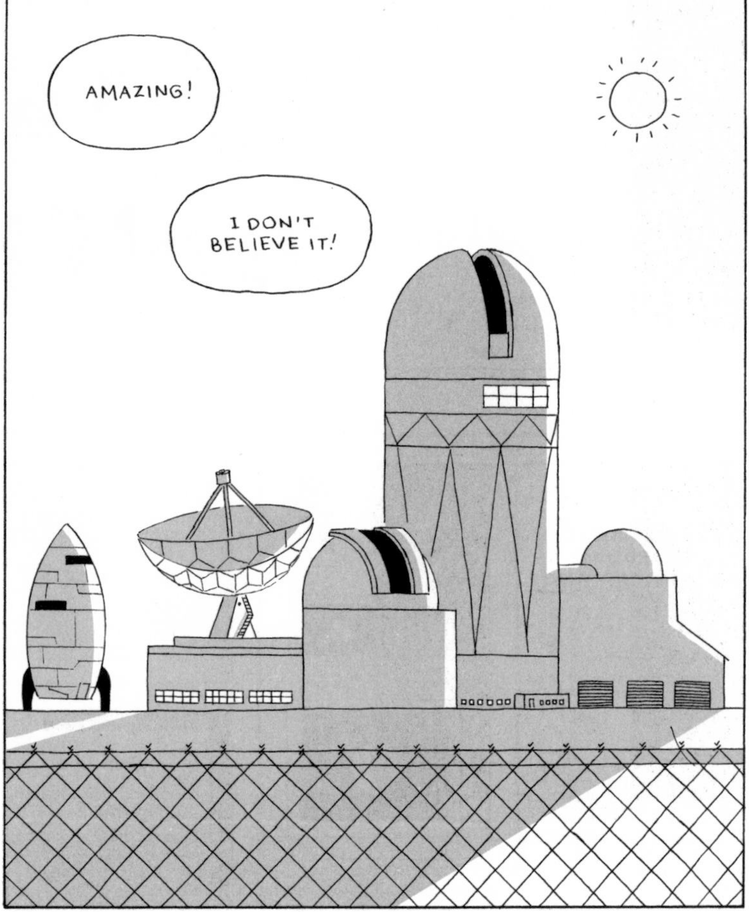
AMAZING!
I DON'T BELIEVE IT!

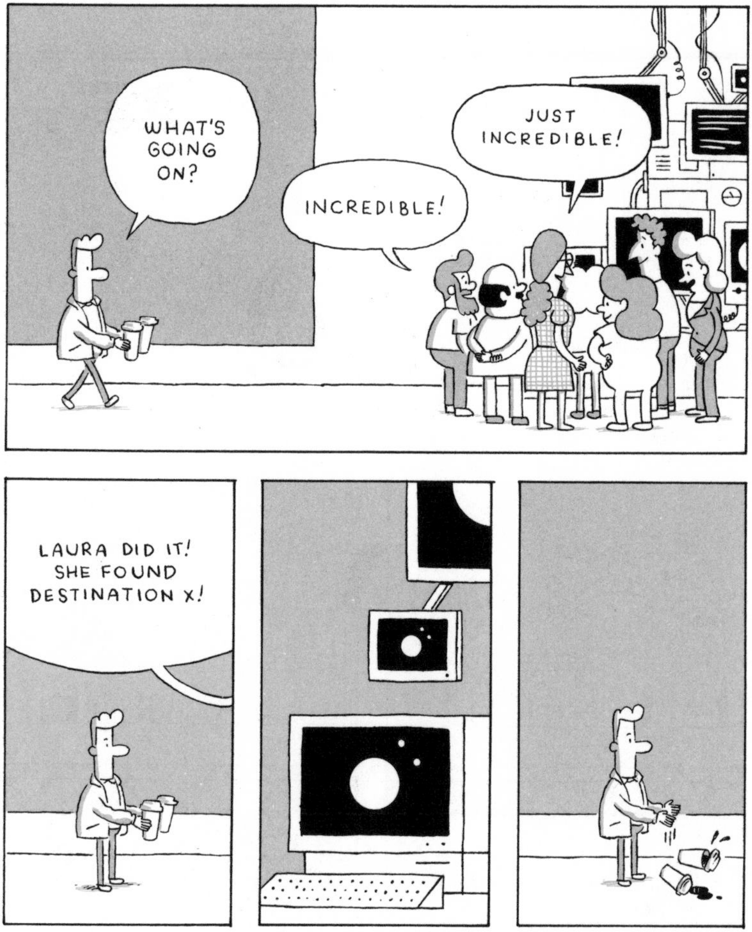
WHAT'S GOING ON?
INCREDIBLE!
JUST INCREDIBLE!
LAURA DID IT! SHE FOUND DESTINATION X!

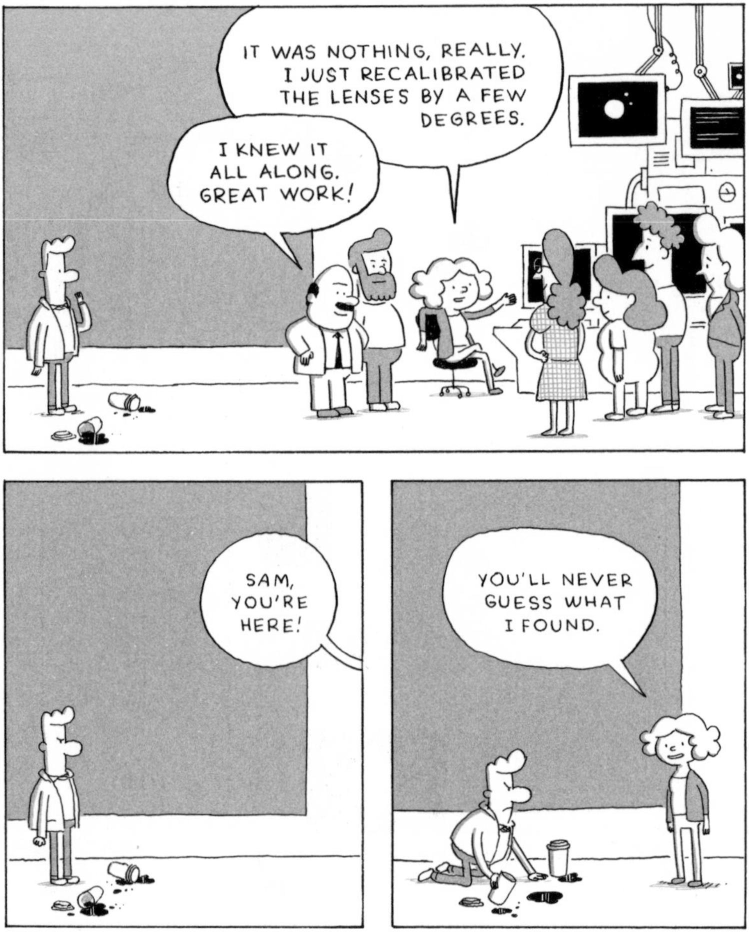
IT WAS NOTHING, REALLY. I JUST RECALIBRATED THE LENSES BY A FEW DEGREES.
I KNEW IT ALL ALONG. GREAT WORK!
SAM, YOU'RE HERE!
YOU'LL NEVER GUESS WHAT I FOUND.

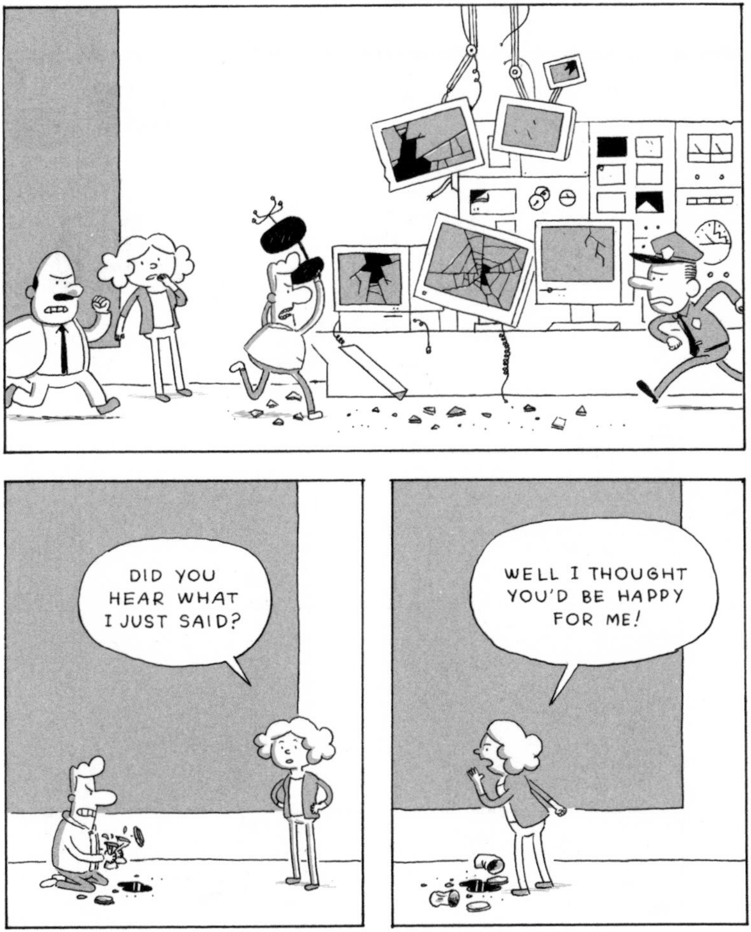
DID YOU HEAR WHAT I JUST SAID?
WELL I THOUGHT YOU'D BE HAPPY FOR ME!

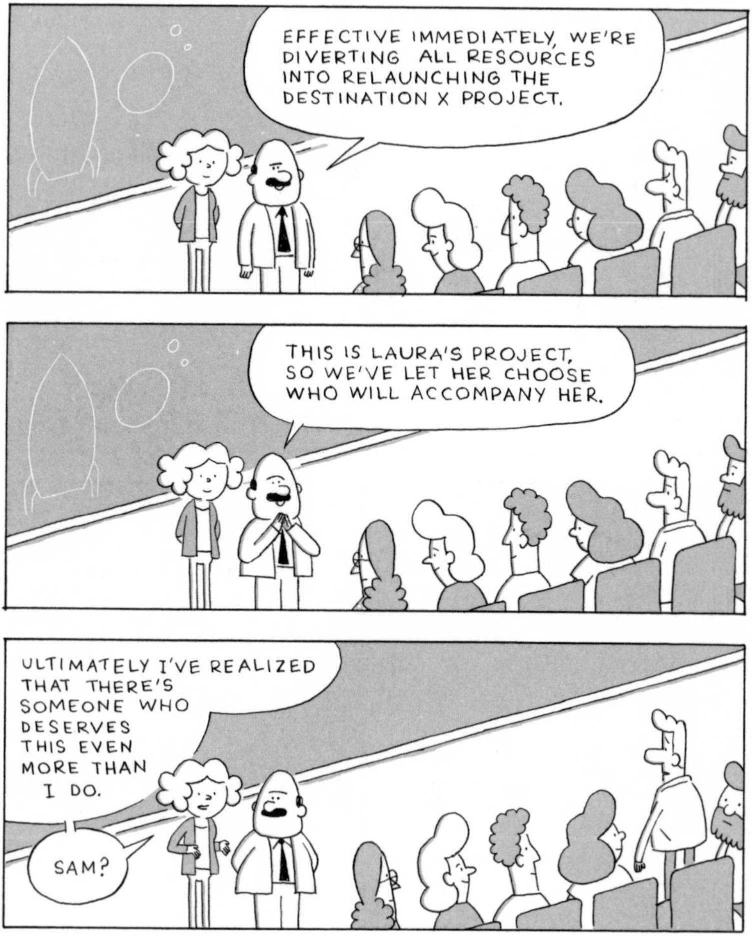
EFFECTIVE IMMEDIATELY, WE'RE DIVERTING ALL RESOURCES INTO RELAUNCHING THE DESTINATION X PROJECT.
THIS IS LAURA'S PROJECT, SO WE'VE LET HER CHOOSE WHO WILL ACCOMPANY HER.
ULTIMATELY I'VE REALIZED THAT THERE'S SOMEONE WHO DESERVES THIS EVEN MORE THAN I DO.
SAM?

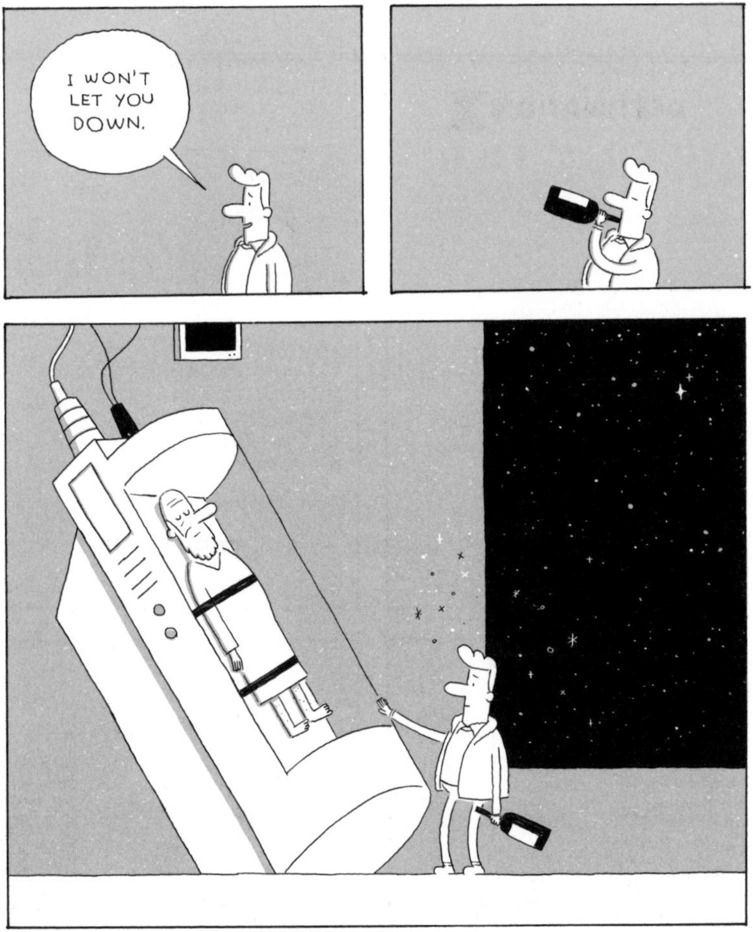
I WON'T LET YOU DOWN.

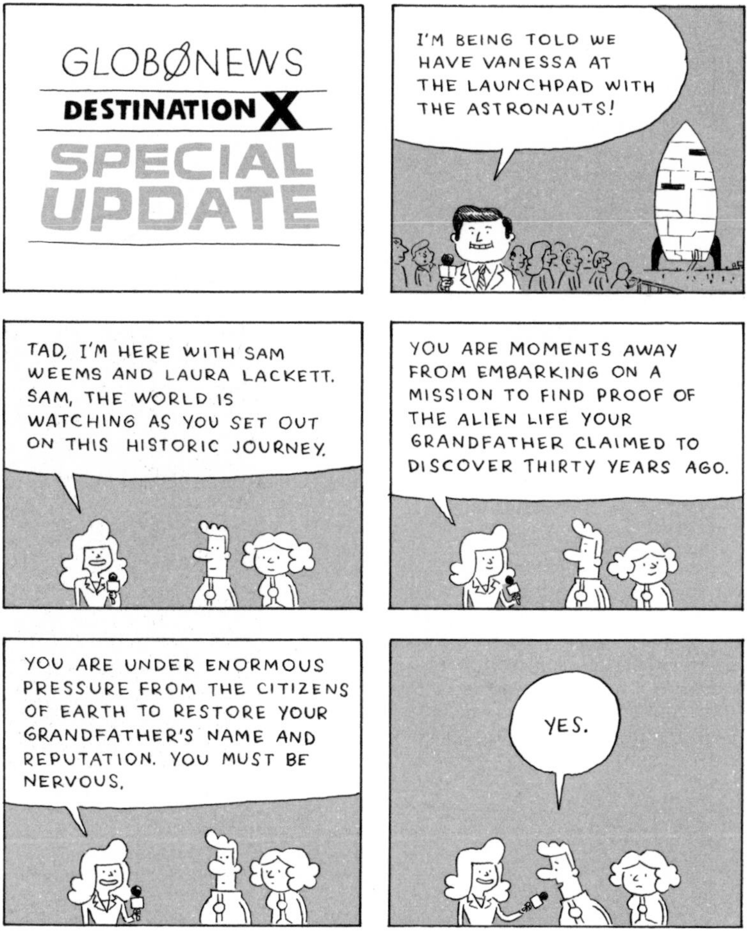
GLOBØNEWS
DESTINATION X
SPECIAL UPDATE
I'M BEING TOLD WE HAVE VANESSA AT THE LAUNCHPAD WITH THE ASTRONAUTS!
TAD, I'M HERE WITH SAM WEEMS AND LAURA LACKETT. SAM, THE WORLD IS WATCHING AS YOU SET OUT ON THIS HISTORIC JOURNEY.
YOU ARE MOMENTS AWAY FROM EMBARKING ON A MISSION TO FIND PROOF OF THE ALIEN LIFE YOUR GRANDFATHER CLAIMED TO DISCOVER THIRTY YEARS AGO.
YOU ARE UNDER ENORMOUS PRESSURE FROM THE CITIZENS OF EARTH TO RESTORE YOUR GRANDFATHER'S NAME AND REPUTATION. YOU MUST BE NERVOUS.
YES.

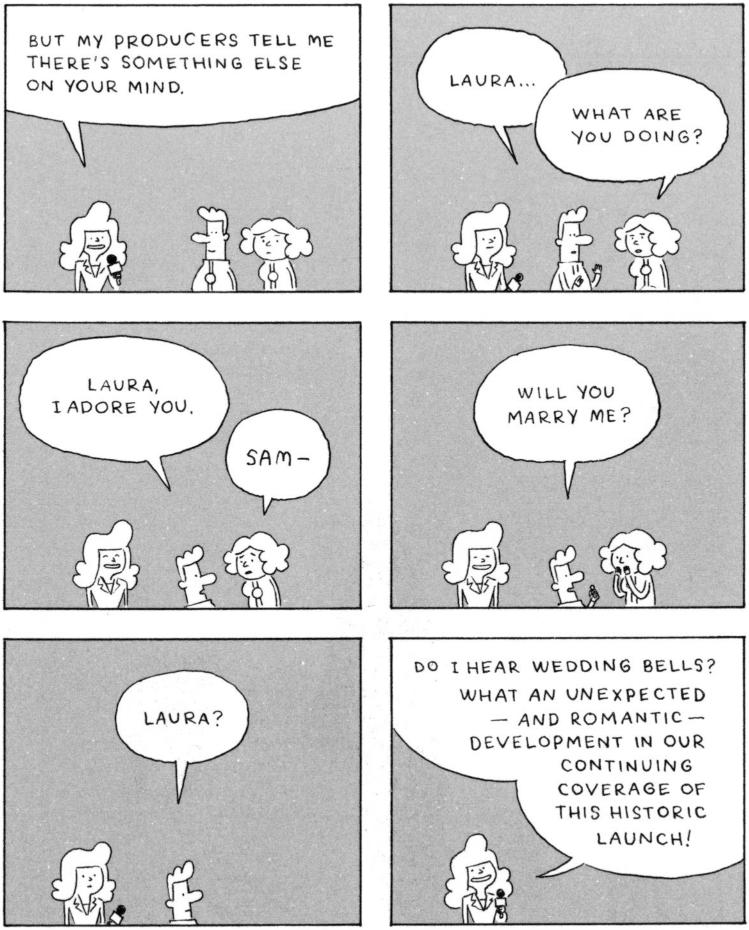
BUT MY PRODUCERS TELL ME THERE'S SOMETHING ELSE ON YOUR MIND.
LAURA...
WHAT ARE YOU DOING?
LAURA, I ADORE YOU.
SAM–
WILL YOU MARRY ME?
LAURA?
DO I HEAR WEDDING BELLS? WHAT AN UNEXPECTED — AND ROMANTIC — DEVELOPMENT IN OUR CONTINUING COVERAGE OF THIS HISTORIC LAUNCH!

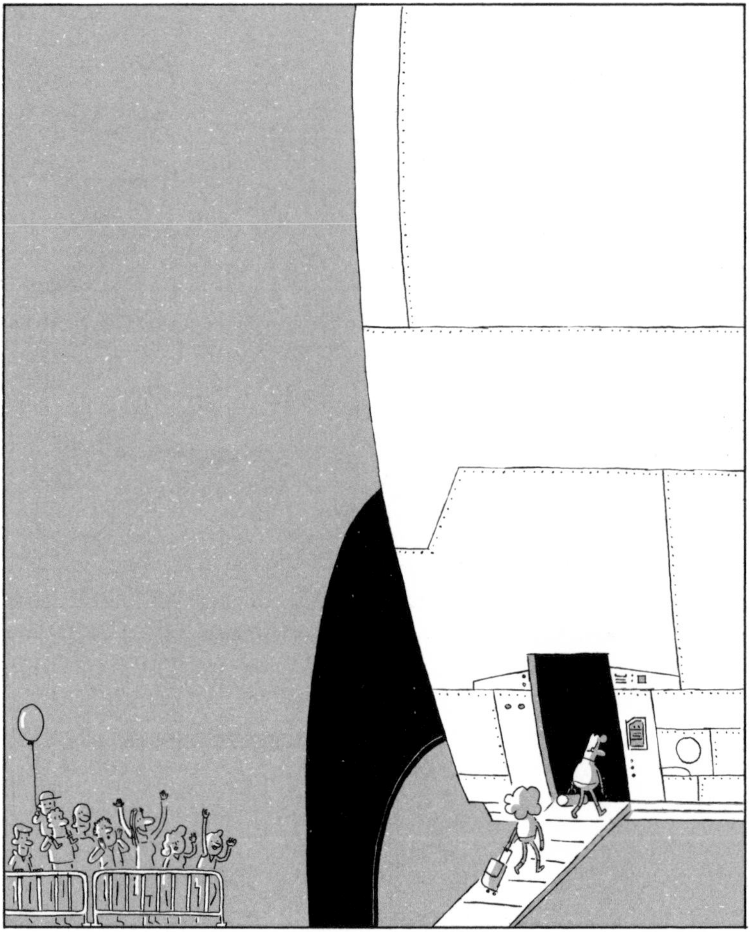

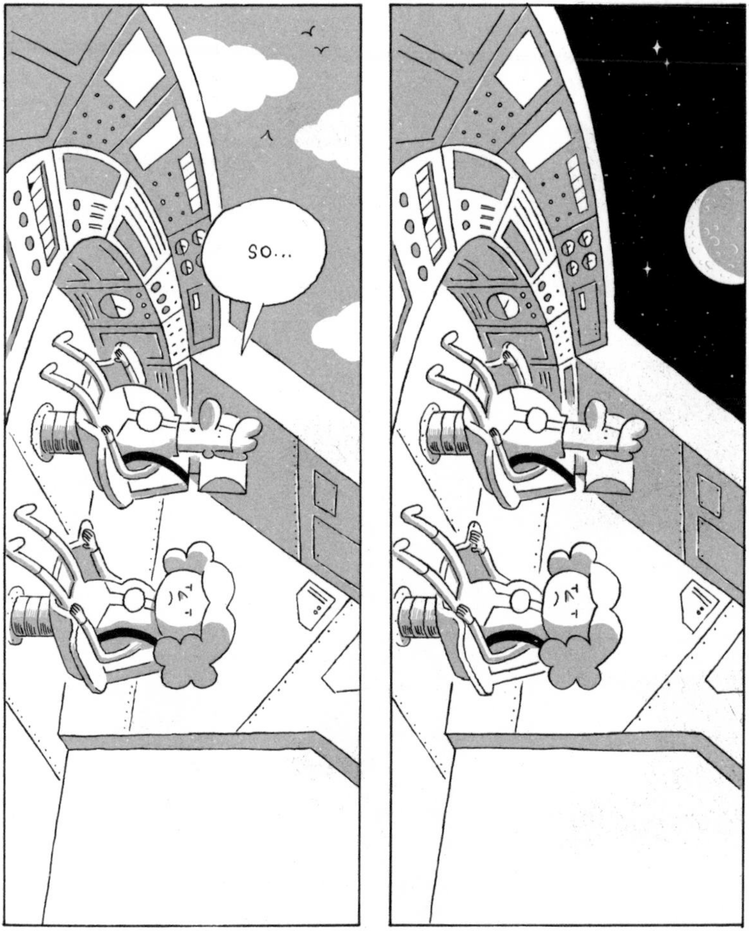
SO...

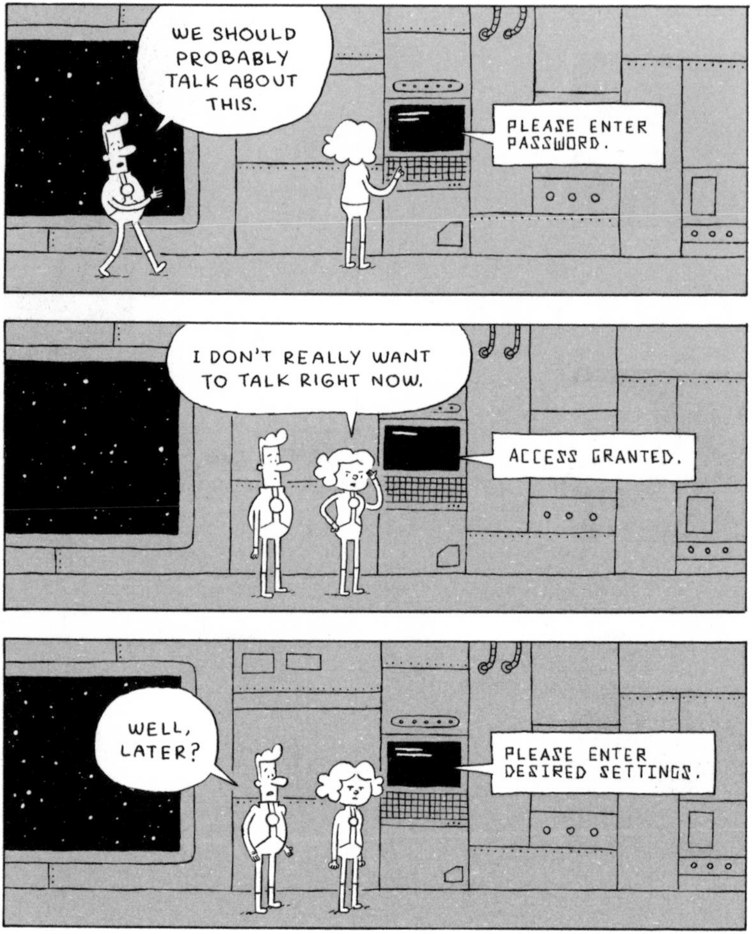
WE SHOULD PROBABLY TALK ABOUT THIS.
PLEASE ENTER PASSWORD.
I DON'T REALLY WANT TO TALK RIGHT NOW.
ACCESS GRANTED.
WELL, LATER?
PLEASE ENTER DESIRED SETTINGS.

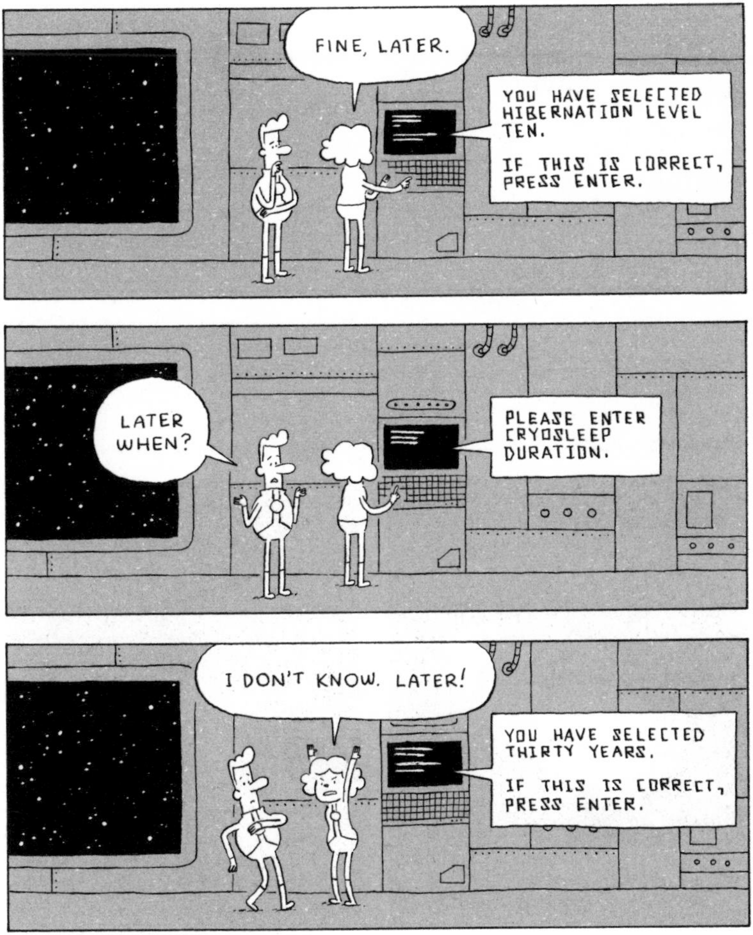
FINE, LATER.
YOU HAVE SELECTED HIBERNATION LEVEL TEN.
IF THIS IS CORRECT, PRESS ENTER.
LATER WHEN?
PLEASE ENTER CRYOSLEEP DURATION.
I DON'T KNOW. LATER!
YOU HAVE SELECTED THIRTY YEARS.
IF THIS IS CORRECT, PRESS ENTER.

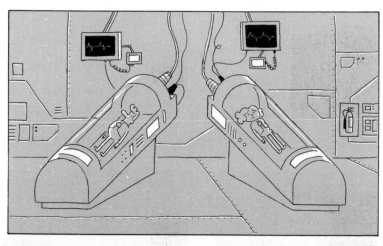

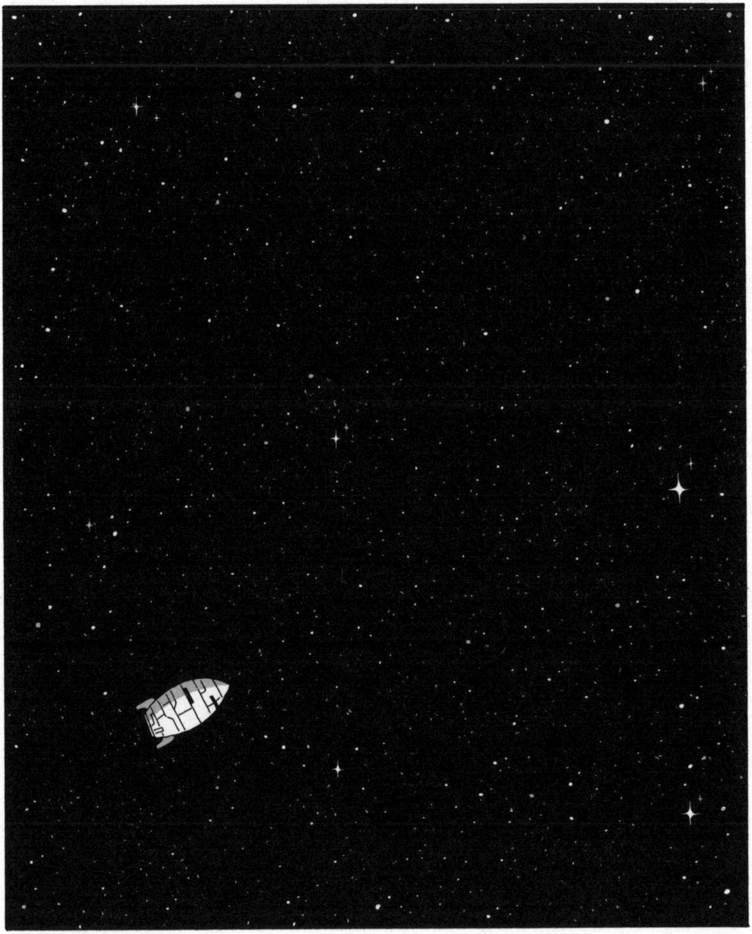

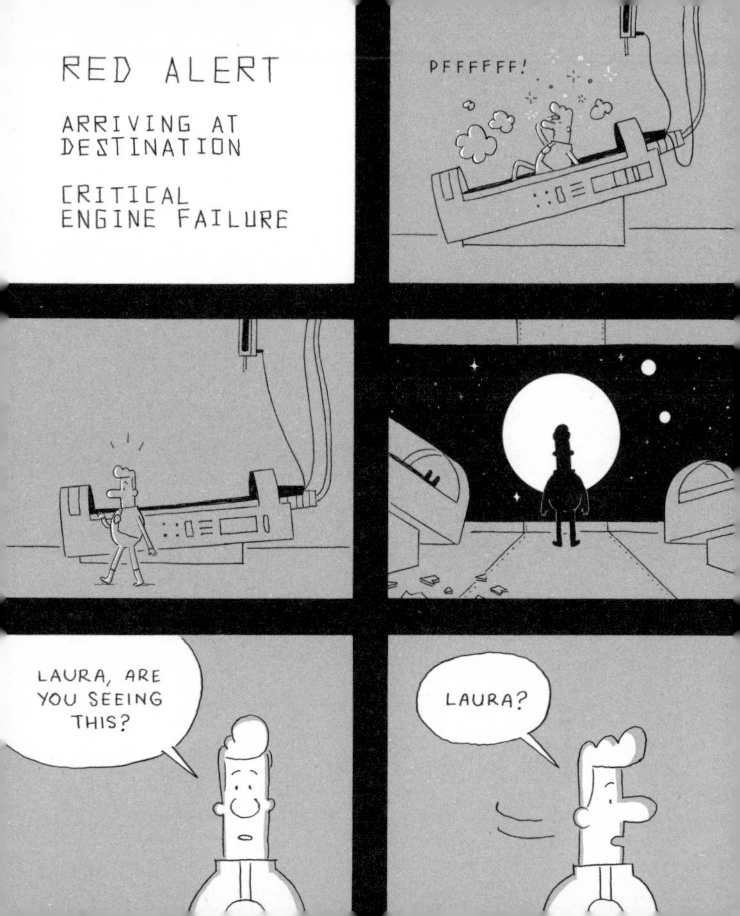
RED ALERT
ARRIVING AT DESTINATION
CRITICAL ENGINE FAILURE
PFFFFFF!
LAURA, ARE YOU SEEING THIS?
LAURA?

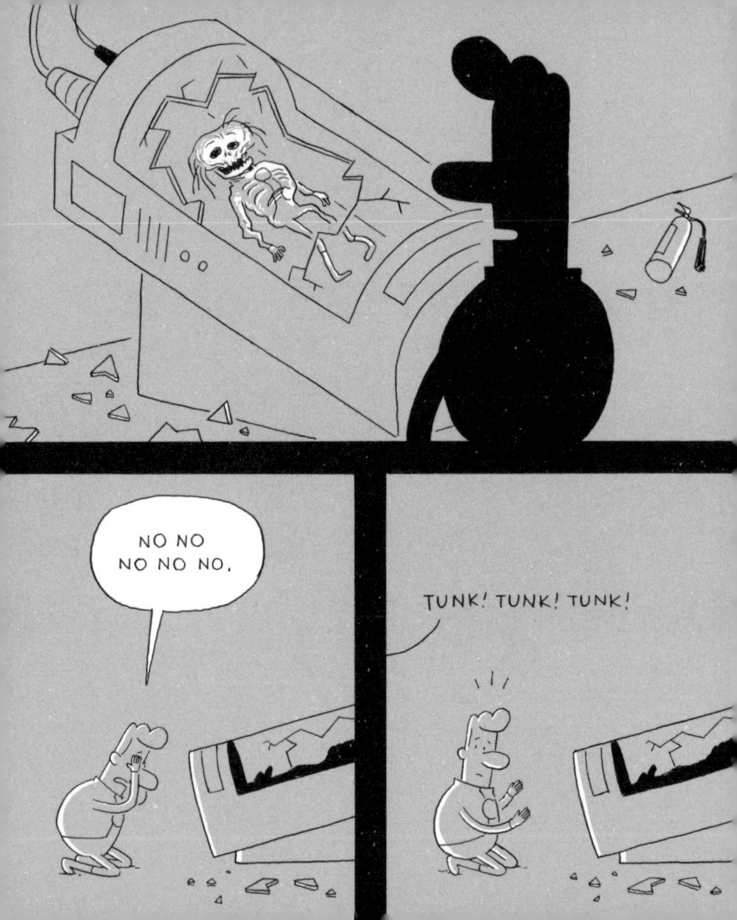
NO NO
NO NO NO.
TUNK! TUNK! TUNK!

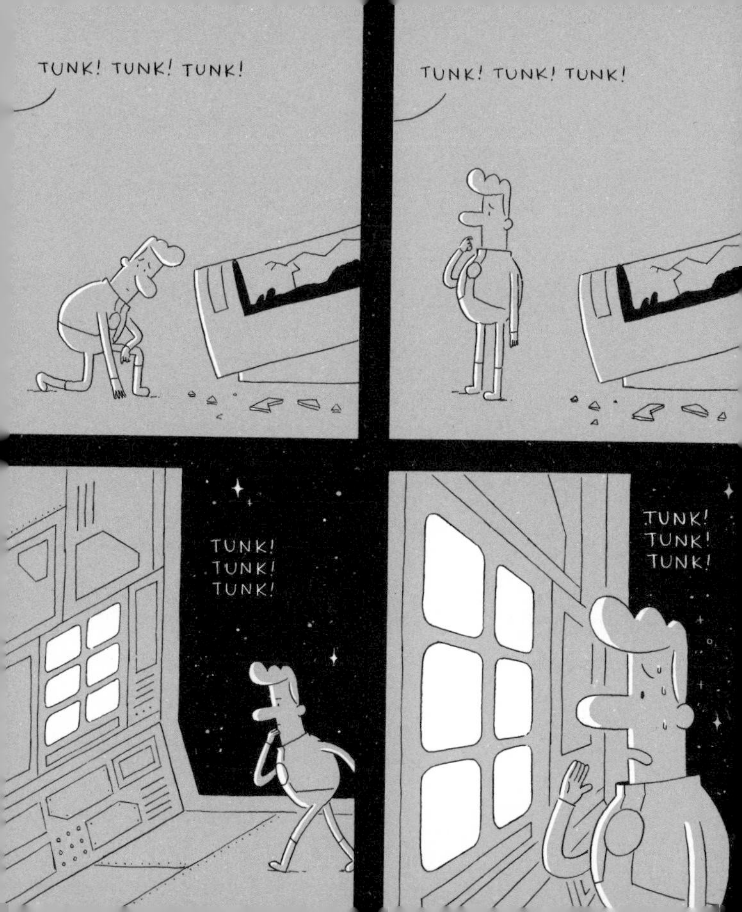
TUNK! TUNK! TUNK!
TUNK! TUNK! TUNK!
TUNK! TUNK! TUNK!
TUNK! TUNK! TUNK!

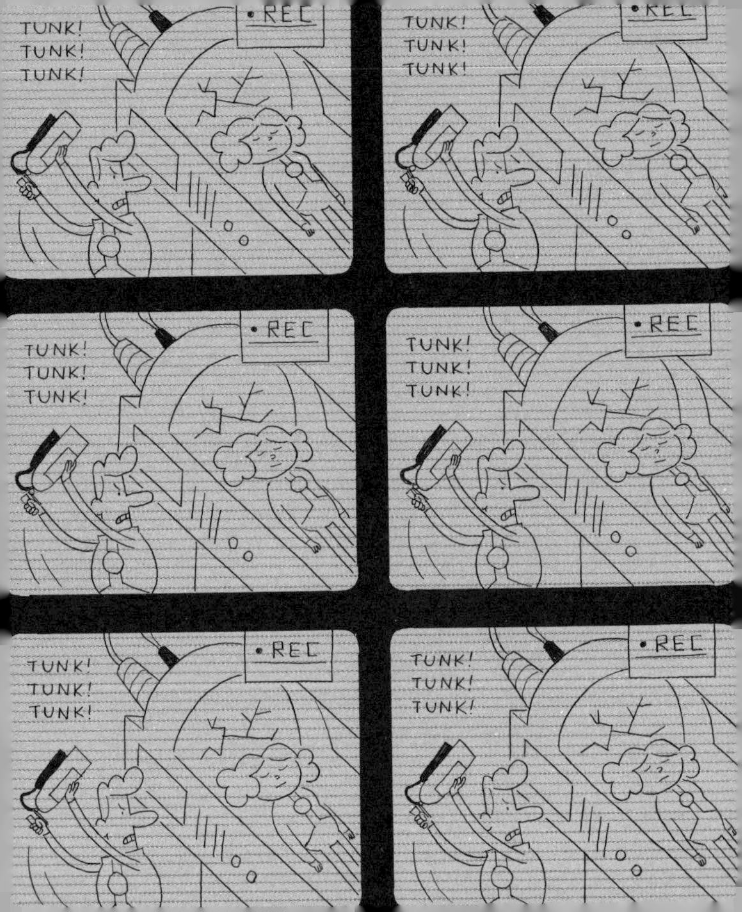
TUNK! TUNK! TUNK!
• REC
TUNK! TUNK! TUNK!
• REC
TUNK! TUNK! TUNK!
• REC
TUNK! TUNK! TUNK!
• REC
TUNK! TUNK! TUNK!
• REC
TUNK! TUNK! TUNK!
• REC

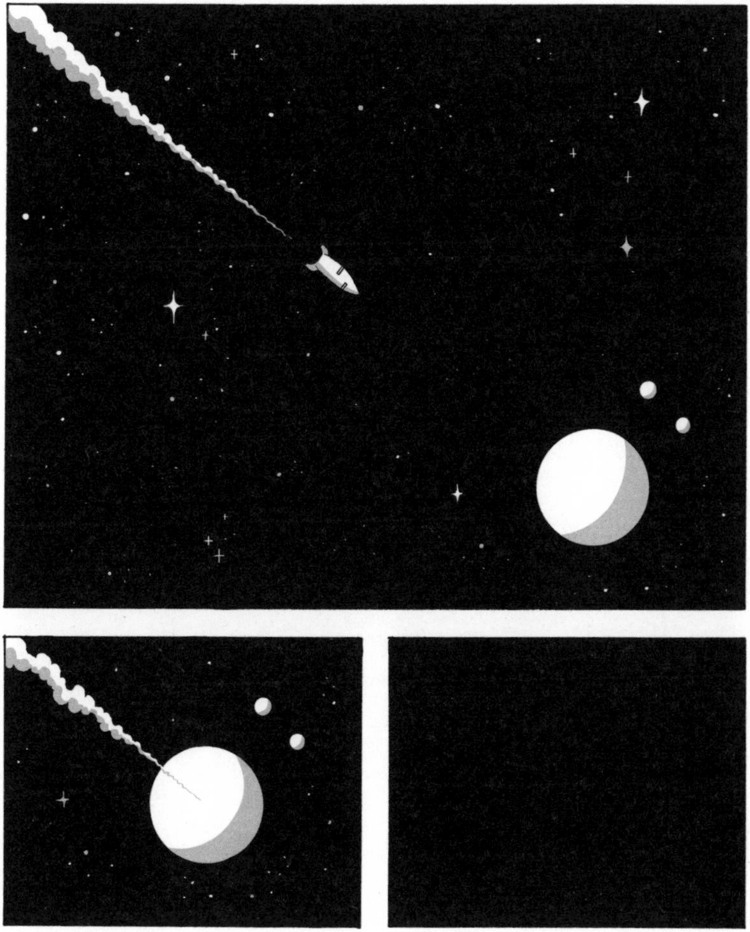

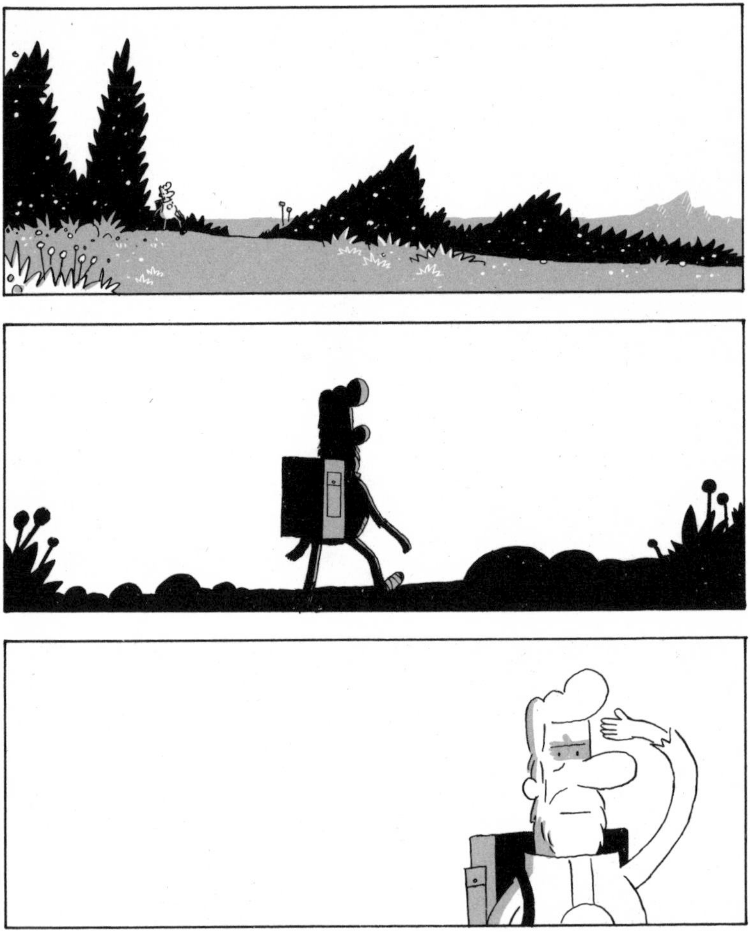

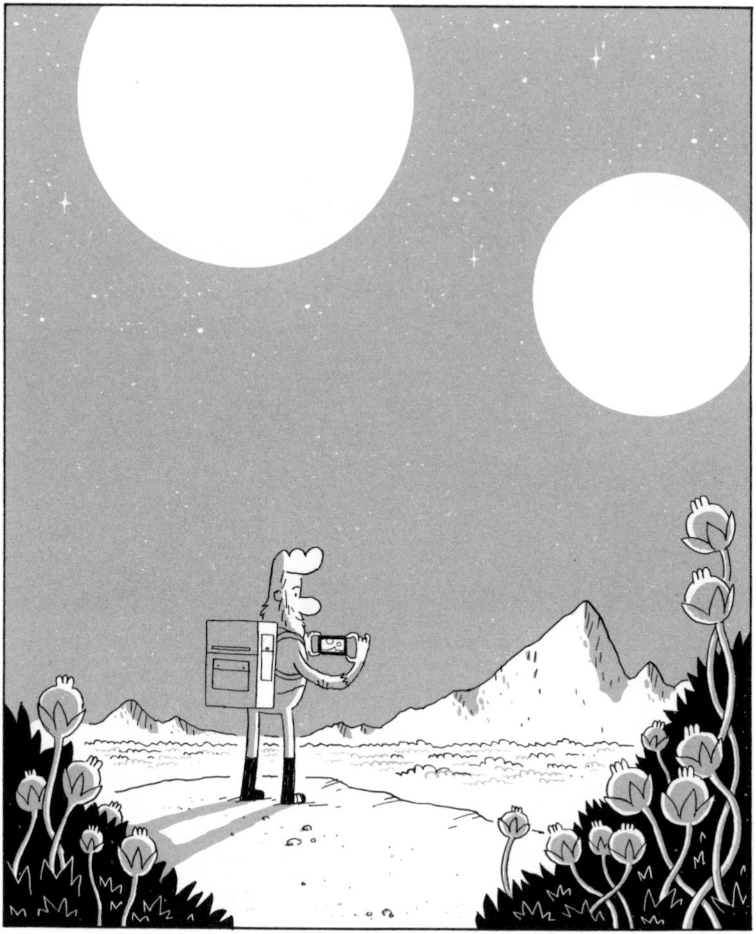

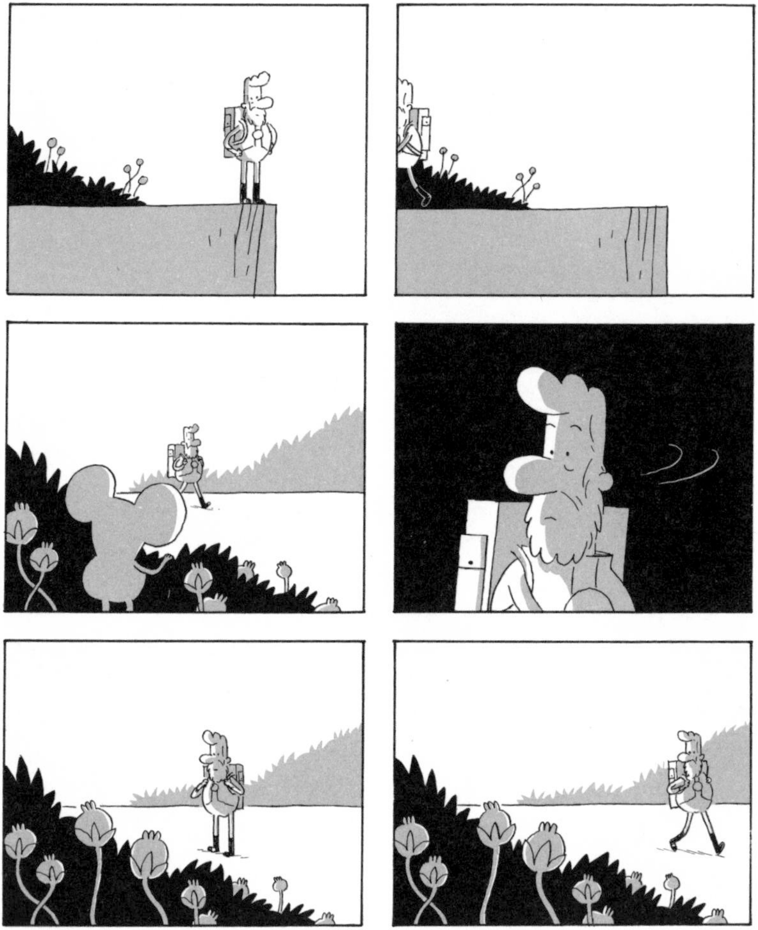

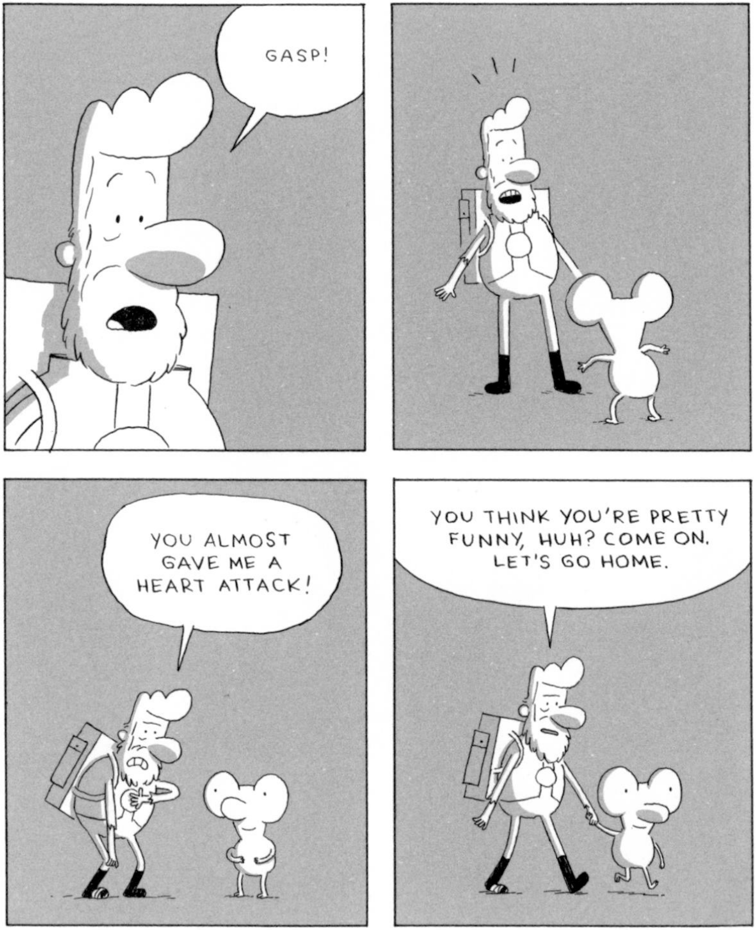
GASP!
YOU ALMOST GAVE ME A HEART ATTACK!
YOU THINK YOU'RE PRETTY FUNNY, HUH? COME ON. LET'S GO HOME.

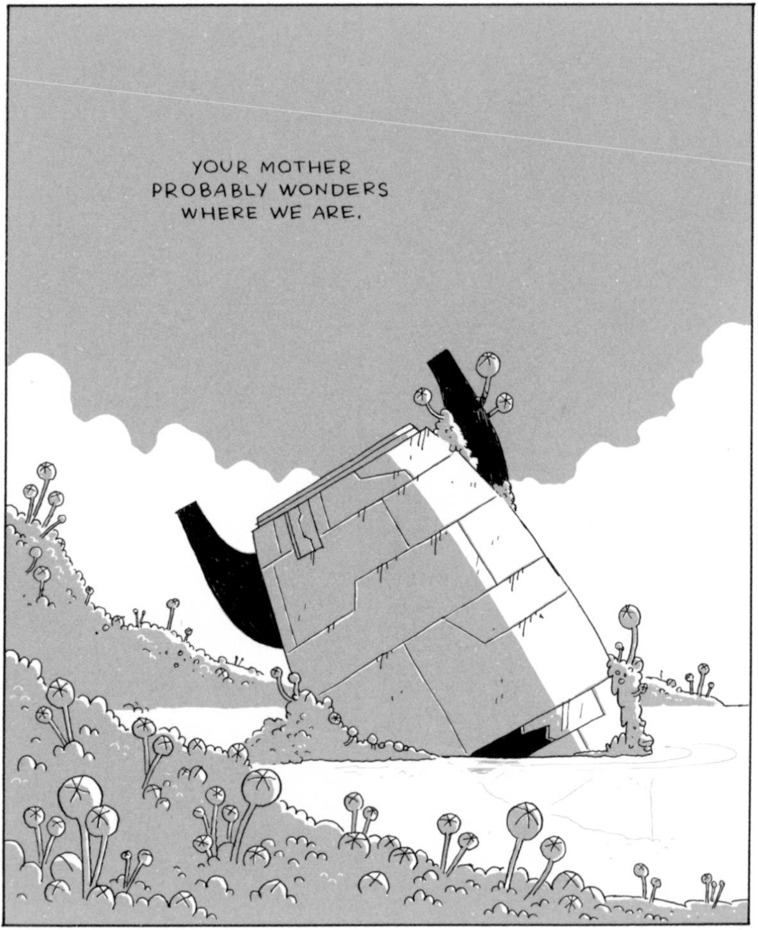
YOUR MOTHER PROBABLY WONDERS WHERE WE ARE.